Personal Volcano

LAURA MORIARTY

NIGHTBOAT BOOKS

NEW YORK

ISBN 978-1-937658-96-0

Design and typesetting by Margaret Tedesco
Text set in Roman Antique and Lora
Cover art Frank Moore, *Study for La Boccetta* III, 2001. Gouache, ink, oil
and watercolor, on Arches paper. Courtesy of the Gesso Foundation.

Cataloging-in-publication data is available
from the Library of Congress

Nightboat Books
New York
www.nightboat.org

Personal Volcano

Contents

I.

Glass Action

MY VOLCANO
takes the form of a mountain or
GLASS ACTION in this case ephemeral as when passion's
end is evident to both lover and other who, fucked from
the beginning, but more determined for the fact of the DISASTER,
answers every day the question of who loses whom or what what when LIFE is no longer
organized around LOVE leaving EARTH and VOLCANOES intact except in dreams which reprise
how it all lived and died in a landscape bereft of everything (one) not left alive

Movement generates SPACE
Catastrophic terrane disruption
A way to name the HOLO
officially now
ANTHROPOCENE
Epoch
Longer than an age
Shorter than a period
Names of times
Including the present
ACCELERATION
Stilled life lay
Awake the last
2.6 million or sixty odd
YEARS
As we change

TERRANE TERRAIN

Current volcanic alert level the same
　　"Terrane" a fragment of earth's crust broken off from one
　　　　and attached to another TECTONIC PLATE.
　　　　　　"Terrain" the vertical and horizontal of land surface, so-called relief/I was relieved
　　　　　　　　saying to myself "this time doesn't exist" though I knew I was caught in it.
　　　　　　　　　　Time not existing meant only that I was not available for the next hour.
　　　　　　　　　　And not at work or being otherwise made or paid or observed
　　　　　　　　　　Mount Konocti, the nearest volcano to my present location
　　　　　　　　　　part of the Clear Lake Volcanic Field
　　　　　　　　　　whose more or less active
　　　　　　　　　　composite dacitic lava dome produced an ashfall 10,000 years ago
　　　　　　　　　Unknown things go off unknowably
　　　　　　　　　And change the EARTH
　　　　　　　　Cretaceous Inland Sea
　　　　　　　Mount Shasta erupted in 1786
　　　　　　Lassen Peak from 1914 to 1921
　　　　　No things without time
　　　　Without warning and in spite of scrutiny and expectation
　　　They take shape "To illustrate how attitudes toward nature can change...
consider the mountain." Yi-Fu Tuan, *Topophilia*

　　Temple MOUNTAIN continuum

　　Ash crafted series of calderas
　　Today we live in a giddily active volcanic regime
　　Crumbs from which LAYER CAKE
　　Taste like memory

　　"Volcanoes of passion" mentioned by my lover during the

open relationship we were attempting to have then.
Gets in eyes and mouth producing TEARS,
coughing, and unbearable sadness.

The Antler and Sonoma Orogenies
Forces and events associated with MOUNTAIN building
Preparation for the TRIP includes choosing a date and
itinerary, researching places to stay, making reservations
deciding what to do there, printing maps, etc.

A seamount in the northwestern Pacific Ocean, the largest volcano
on Earth, could rival the largest in the solar system—the mighty Olympus Mons on Mars
whose gradual rise might not however excite much interest if you were there.

Beyond being on MARS
Happy again

The artist experiences the LIGHT and speaks about it in the library he built
A tectonic and temporal analog

Fragments less than a tenth of an inch across of minerals and ASH
along with gas ascend forming a huge, billowing eruption column and, eventually, cloud.

"And roll'd along the ground"

HOLLOW EARTH

No permanence meaning no Eternalls but time everywhere going in the same direction
Lead melting in hollowed out clouds and other theories of lightning that proved

In 1335 Petrarch climbed Mount Vesuvius
The invisible hand appears
Originally meaning the ECONOMY
or here NATURE or even GOD
to be false

> An exploration of what can happen next
> *nuées ardentes*
> Alternative temporality
> Human-relevant timescale
> *How To Build a Volcano*

> If ROCK is like BONE or one becomes the other over time
> These ossuaries
> "Seismic scream portends volcanic activity"

> These orogenies
> whose forces include much that
> begins and ends

> from the tip of your nose to the top of the Transamerica PYRAMID
> man-made volcanic form
> a system whose time is short but seems long

But where are we in all this stone?
> Time stretching out behind
and before meaning ahead into
> interval, period, personal history, ecstatic
> hour, rate of marching, mood, existence, or job
to mention the worst and best of duration as experience

when a specific contract with reference to prevailing
        conditions seeming endless nevertheless
        ENDS

                    Peak of wonder
                a new thing for the eyes but old also
            reading applied to rocks, minerals, stuck together
        we stick together FLEXURE occurs below and among us travelling
    variously to places where objects, this pebble, saved by me gets in everything as
  for example ash or hot wind blows into and around us when leaving Mount Pelée which
exploded in 1902 you and I not there then but later looking back and chose that moment

pictured by me
                    as memorial
to yourself on your book
                    not dead yet
                    then dead
doors where mourning occurs in those shots shown also as open to the sea
crockery, columns, items smashed, suspended
in EARTH

        The disaster table
        in our house on Jackson Street
        another house another Jackson Street
        another HOUR spent walking through
        the forest on the upper reaches of the mountain
        another mountain covered with ASH as if
        ASH meant nothing

                              Mineralized pages bound or
                           forged forced to dig through
                        loose GRAVEL to the thing destroyed
                     Take away this earth the artist said or
                  "author" of this book that it was too late
               Goodbye sadness he cried out as one who was
Monumentally difficult though not in that in PLACE

      THERE in Oakland where now
We talk about your FACE
      "for wind is air"

Or FLAME years since
Oakland Fire at the Oakland Museum display
      of a traffic jam
      wind driving flames
      around those who presumably got out
      but did they?

From across the bay we saw the ASH CLOUD
      familiar now
      maculated dark
      pine tree column as younger Pliny wrote
      his uncle went into it forever
      fire raining down
      first letter
      not OMEN
      disaster itself

Is this a geological cataclysm
    or one of the spirit or body?
    whose throat and mouth is the word for entrance hall
      fauces a term given by Vitruvius to
        narrow passages on either of the
          tablinum through which access would be
            obtained from the *atrium* to the *peristylar*
              Earth or MOUNTAIN as house: old idea
                body as plant i.e. throat of calyx, portion
                  of spiral shell you look into and hear

      Your FACE fair not as light but
      lit like Moses with his God on
      full of grace or space

Everyone looks away

2.

Erupting Light

The cratological meaning
Force of the stars pressing

terrestrial OBJECTS down
Pliny the Elder believed

he could survive the pyroclastic
eruption of Vesuvius that

twisted the citizens of Pompeii
into casts of DYING as

going into this storm of stone
his doomed boat

whose sailors his servants
had a terrible day at WORK

Wife and nephew
watching the PINE TREE CLOUD

rise into the stratosphere
turning day into night

Vesuvius erupting dark one could have said
as now listening to "ERUPTING LIGHT"

by an Icelandic cellist
composing the weight of the stars

not heavier near the top of the world
which has no top or bottom

though it can be said
that PUMICE floats and OBSIDIAN doesn't

Glass action notwithstanding
it is difficult to act

Sulfur is brimstone
Sulfur dioxide makes ACID RAIN

heats the atmosphere, pollutes the air and
preserves dried fruit

Sulfur is mined hydraulically not by digging.
Jupiter's moon Io owes its color

to SULFUR as does the deadly gas
used in the Great War

The sulfur poem
The sulfur dioxide poem

Poem of FRACKING

"Natural gas plays a key role in our nation's clean energy future." EPA begins their online article
of potential dangers of fracking. FRACK. Their foregone conclusion dismisses the inevitable
failure adequately to treat wastewater and

fugitive emissions of methane and
reliance on carbon based energy and

delaying the move toward
wind and sun

But what of the BIRDS
chewed up by the turbines

as I stare up at them
in my mind as often when

I want to drive or fly or otherwise
use up the LIGHT

created long ago
as things & PEOPLE BURNED

to produce the exact situation
in which we find

not so much the human as
the social and economic condition

ENCLOSED ENTOMBED

in which the asymmetrical concentration
of wealth once common as DIRT

not free like the SUN
and anyway

solar power never
but what is ever enough?

And can we, as we thought NOT, cause a VOLCANIC ERUPTION if through the effects of global warming the pressure on the earth's mantle is changed? Will anthropo-seismic events occur? have occurred? Humans certainly cause earthquakes, as shown by those that swarm through FRACKED Texas and elsewhere.

"Geology," Humphry Davy wrote, "perhaps more than any other department of natural philosophy, is a science of contemplation."

The IMPERIAL Enlightenment
brought about by that thinking

is this HOLLOW SCENE
also called CAPITALISM

but isn't as well lit as
donated LAMPS illuminating

the Emma Goldman/Silvia
Federici/bell hooks Room

occupied by a small
but tender nonhierarchical

and yet finally
male-dominated commune

in that nonplace
of PERSONAL REVOLUTION

which ends again
or doesn't really end

and yet from which
as usual one finds oneself

so gone

3.

Road Trip

The great machine of the world
not TECTONICS not God not
"disordered chance" not proving
"The sun has four differences"

But invasive permanent
sleepless and war-like

"I am action" one says meaning HEAT
is ALIVE a geological form communicates
telluric currents or volcanic strife
travelling great distances via obscure agents

TECTONIC WARFARE

Volcano called active as individual
activist having an impact on
the global COMMONS or on uses
of despair, desire, suffering

and utopia found as we approach
the mountain as people not dead yet
I think of you or
TIME OF THE OTHER (you me)
Mountains not infinite
Hope not ours
"Never stop on a crumbling slope."
Admonition obvious until

Preparing for another road trip
North or in this case South
What does it matter where you go?
And yet of course each moment
strangely noticeable and equal
to nothing like itself ourselves
formed by the crisis we grow
from or to which respond
moving through some ecstatic
notion until we run like the simple
through the streets said to have screamed
JUDGMENT DAY though others don't but who were they?
not to be simple in the FACE of catastrophe?
A SAINT was seen to stave off the PYROCLASTIC
CLOUD as we might say now but that was a BAROQUE eruption
as unlike the multiple forms of the POST VOLCANO as we are like
you in your bastion (for WE are unhappy) unsurprising yet unstoppable
Red in the old sense of what comes together urgent
in the flow of things and time
We are on our way to a mountain
I see in our mind
A dynamic interface where physical, chemical,
biological, and human processes cause and are affected by
EARTHLY forces and systems
It's a great plan and each time
we go away I wonder why
I am not always gone
This time South but dreaming North
hot but cold toward a massive caldera or not there
but on the side of or close to an imagined volcanic Los Angeles

not subductive as would be required tectonically but simply
the ferocity of a great city blasting in all directions

stands in for the state of disaster
or dissatisfaction asking finally
can you get there from here?
Where nothing has erupted since before
people learned to write though then
rhyolite poured across the ground
at highway speeds and clouds of steam
dropped ASH like snow and collapsed
into the empty magma chamber

While real volcanoes as Mount Lassen far
to the north called earlier Lassen Peak
remnant of nameless mountains
named in retrospect Maïdo and Tehama after
people but not by or with them accrue as
ridges in mid ocean grow at the same
rate as fingernails and hair then erupt
taking everything out as unburned trees
are killed by heat in separate cases
both part of the remnants of the Cascades
we have from unimaginably long
ago left as we are in the extreme present

where on 5 North we pass
Black Butte to the east Mount
Lassen Woods Starlight

Pines Rock Creek
Tehama Caldera
always in view Eskimo Hill
Summit 5,900 ft.
glimpse of Lassen
Hat Creek North Battle
Ground Creek Lassen
through trees devastated
area destroyed in 1915
like yesterday eruption
waxing gibbous snow visible
Prospect Volcano cinder cone
erupted 1666 plug dome
puzzled rocks quenched blobs
survival forest Chaos Jumbles
Let's stay here now listen to
the Acorn Stomp retire early
with migraine rise early
pack up go on to Hat Creek
Radio Observatory
Cruiseamerica.com
McKinney Waltz, Shasta, and Lassen
on respective horizons
Cinder Pot Road large dust devil
Tornado volcano continuum
Hat Creek Corporate Headquarters
Volcano Song Meredith Monk
You Are Wherever Your Thoughts Are
Steve Reich Pandora the town

Siskiyou County Line North on 89
Dead Horse Summit 4500 ft.
Shasta Trinity National Forest
Volcanic Legacy Highway
Medicine Lake corridor
Knockin' on Heaven's Door
Well within the blast zone
The presence of volcanoes
seems to slow down time

As to travel's being imperial she thought
It always was or almost a demonstration
as much as a talk no geology
but in things she thought as in
the right moment to be seen when
one feature towers over everything
the parallax view emerges from the horizon
like a ghost sinks back and reappears
taking over half the sky as we drive
around the active zone like short lived flies
among the stone giants changeable as
they are as geological features go
off among us

Shasta covered in snow but not enough
resplendent in drought
The state dissolves into dust we breathe every day
particles don't melt but cling
are coughed out or not

The body of the other in time
One's own body Own time

The encounter and infusion of irregular
forms infiltrate in imprecise, unrepeatable,
imperfect, and continuous ways

Mental activity compressed into the PRESENT
disidentification said to come from no memories
No memories never occurring
at least not yet
Jays in trees in the yard finches
also golden orioles
used to be NATURE
Thickening of infospheric crust
AIR OF EARTH never was
but is now

"A universal fog fatal and morbid
obscures the northern part of the world"

Benjamin Franklin commented about Hekla in Iceland in his meteorological paper of May 1784—
the year of David's *Oath of the Horatii*, just before the French Revolution and the year the
Treaty of Paris officially ends the Revolutionary War
the year also of the Laki eruption
        in Iceland not a single event so much as
            months of lava flows and explosions
                eject enough basaltic LAVA
                    to pave Boston, San Francisco or

not quite all of Oakland
releasing sulphur dioxide infused
acid rain on grasses and cattle
producing ten thousand deaths
called the HAZE FAMINE
a summer which did not come
and if happened now would produce
a few years of cold, air travel disruption,
crop failure, and other CONSEQUENCES
as expected with what would be
the largest flow of so-called
ANTHROPOCENE

Volcanic eruptions as ephemeral
moments or MONUMENTS
fracture related events also called
nonlinear sequences where
hierarchy, scale, networks
of cracks and broken pieces
are part of a dynamics that
ACCELERATES until after the catastrophe
structural links satisfy the power flow
as much as it can be satisfied
A return to pre-catastrophic value
occurs while extreme ANTHROTURBATION
continues comprising simply
transfer of carbon from rock to atmo
altering the WORLD while crystal mush
below the surface continues to cool and

occasionally ERUPTS adding substance
to the planet filled will plants and animals
only not so many as before
and not us

"Every day a struggle and today no different
We fight to make things right and cure ourselves"
Vincent Medina on tape at the Big Break Visitors Center

Renegade Radio WE DARE YOU TO LISTEN
Crater filled with coyote bush, sage,
branches, bones, volcanic darkness
Mantle plumes meander and deflect
like the delta of a river as they merge
with the less viscous upper mantle rock
anchored at the boundary with the core
as Hawaii or Yellowstone stolen places
as what place isn't in some sense

Life has no choice
but to respond to these
RANDOM COSMOLOGICAL FORCES
animal past animal future territory and body, life, death
invisible powers of EARTH dynamize and impact creating no demand or
objective around which to cohere though opportunistic masses, self-referential
inward-directed processes produce disequilibria, rapid remobilization anyway

These plucky zircons preserve this activity
under Lassen Peaks and Chaos Crags
while on the surface it looks like nothing is happening

4·
Outer East Bay

Where magma no longer
comes up as lava
the time gone
so far back into what
could not be perceived
so seems not to be (but is) real as
we ACCELERATE unlike certain
trees or other things we claim are
inanimate OBJECTS as COMETS
or VOLCANOES produce a no-analog
state in the dynamics and function of
the EARTH or UNIVERSE where
our LABOR also ACCELERATED replaces
the self abandoned long ago
though taken back up now
with ice core levels of CO_2
or other clues to the end of the world.
Momentum builds when
one friend says 50 the other
100 years until ECONOMIC and
CLIMATE collapse will . . .
but what will it do
when the beginning ENDS?
And are they friends only
in the physical rather than
the geophysical sense?
These chosen OBJECTS are anomalies
of critical state and non-linear
time-sequence fracture-related

events which will PERSIST though we
lie down in front of trains and trucks
listening to POISON seep out of the EARTH
which brings us to IRREVERSIBILITY
when the trains are not needed because
oil is cheap though dear and we or
someone who like us is an ANIMAL
screams in the wilderness before
the eruption darkens the EARTH
hot then cold then hot again
Goldilocks or gold itself also present amidst
these changes pours into a gilded
stream which the EPA says will not hurt us

This tea made from the Sacramento River
to which we switched last March from reservoirs
because of the drought and leaves from India
and also China. I can see the Chevron Refinery
from this window also the Port of Richmond
two imperial walkers, a tanker and a derelict boat
off the coast of the San Pablo Bay Yacht Club
ironically named neighborhood of houseboats and
a bar no better than it should be you can find
down a steep slope on a nice day
in the outer East Bay

5.

Invisible Sun

Volcanoes are endangered
not only as worlds but as *the world*
conflict between deep and social ecology,
people, places, things

Volcanic fire buried like breath
A mountain seems not to be but to
represent but then emerges meaningless
in triumph over beauty and thought
relaxing as sitting (mountain again)
with fact of it as back aches or feet sleep

Volcanoes, sublime but domestic, observed
often on vacation, so implicitly part of
work, are not endangered but impose risk
on their surroundings and constituents
involving us in concepts of deep time (related to
deep ecology in being oblivious to the social therefore
coming from a privileged position with regard to actual
time) but then erupt into the present more predictable
than earthquakes but less than storms not unlike wild fire
or lightning which can be part of their bag of tricks.

Why not anthropomorphize?
Lava that appears in dreams
lava of mad people
lava of *One Million Years BC,*
Volcano, Mysterious Island, Pompeii,
Dante's Peak, Journey to the Center of the Earth,
20,000 Leagues Under the Sea

"Where are we?" I asked.

"In the very heart of an extinct volcano, the interior of which has been invaded by the sea, after some great convulsion of the earth."

Volcanoes emblematic of the tropics or of Far North, the Aleutians, the Ring of Fire, of Iceland, of Africa. Kilimanjaro, easily older than humans, looks the same or similar as it looked to first peoples travelling in connected family groups searching for food, headed everywhere.

Earliest remains of humans come from
volcanic regions of Africa and Indonesia.
Bones rapidly covered by ash fall and other
volcanic deposits.

Anaxagoras proposed that eruptions
were caused by great winds stored inside EARTH.
Seneca saw volcanoes as giant furnaces
in which fossil fuels burned—coal,
bitumen, sulfur. Plato that motion generates
heat. Descartes that EARTH was once a SUN.
only smaller and therefore cooler.
Alchemists then Robert Hooke suggest chemical
reaction as Iron with Sulphur are the source of volcanism,
which, the chemical theory of terrestrial heat,
was a dead end hypothesis. There were Neptunists
(basaltic sediments come from ocean) and Plutonists
(basalt is volcanic). Plutonist victory settled the
origin of basalt, leading to recognition of lava

flows and petrology, the study of rock,
crystallization and melting.

Rocks solid but changing liquefy spontaneously
if they move to a region of lower pressure or close
to EARTH's surface. Large scale slow moving currents.
Convective flow. 1904 discovery that radioactive
elements provide heat source for same. (Curie connection.)

Bronze Age eruption of Santorini or Thera
1650 BC where Jerry (Estrin) went in 1974 the winter and
spring before we moved in together and where he
met a German virgin, Ulrike. They got pregnant and
experienced the resulting abortion together in Germany,
Munich, I think, before he returned to me and San Francisco.
I believe it was his only pregnancy. Often in dreams
Jerry is about to go away or has gone or has just
returned. We visited the ruins of Saint Pierre on
Martinique where a pyroclastic flow from Mount
Pelée caused total devastation in 1902. Here he is
pictured there among the other dead.

"A volcano is not made on purpose to frighten
superstitious people into fits of piety nor to
overwhelm devoted cities with destruction." James Hutton,
Scottish doctor, called the Father of Geology.

In 71 BC's Revolt of the Gladiators they hide out in
Vesuvius which provides a natural fortress
but are besieged by Gaius Claudius Glaber

whose men descend the cliffs by wild vines taking
the gladiators by surprise. Later during an eruption
statues nearby crack, a flock of sheep is lost
and people wander unable to help themselves.

Athanasius Kircher's *Mundus Subterraneus*.
His Rococo renditions of Vesuvius. Volcanoes
as alchemists' furnaces finely printed.

"Life is a pure flame and we live by
an invisible SUN within us." Thomas Browne, *Hydriotaphia*

Ambiguities of syntax mirror our situation
our concrete inner history when
a woman is also a man because she
occupies the subject position of scientist
or because she is overflowing with
meaning which also inherits the world.

Volcanoes communicate with the molten
interior of EARTH and the atmosphere
that envelopes the oxidized crust of the planet.

A green volcano is intimated by the red hair of
Arlene Dahl who in green suit, hat and gloves and with
matching parasol claims her place among the
explorers (a widow's right). Her cloak is taken
up by wind on the high ridge as they wait
while the light of a particular day
reveals the way to the inner world.

6.

Verne

The end of all voyages
Known and unknown worlds
A *Treaty of Transcendental Crystallography*
In May my uncle the mineralogist
whose velvet armchair, samples,
and sanctum by Iceland blasted
in thought with ash where crops
and lava also everywhere poor ones
rent themselves as guides to tourists.
Enter Hans. Enter his duck. We dream of them
but see my Uncle, Professor Lidenbrock,
and myself, Axel, decipher an artifact of
Arne Sakmussen. His alchemist's
experiments of ice, rotting, mutability,
astrality and *luco*, a sacred wood, a sea,
anger, cruelty, *craterem*, earth, blood, rose
rushing upward with violence, stupifaction,
and terror, the volcano in his head
in mine. Chance the key. Descend bold
traveler into the crater of Snæfellsjökull
and attain the center of the earth
as I have done, Sakmussen.

The cipher per third atlas on second shelf
and planned expedition when
fainting a woman fixes
the gaze of nephew Axel myself
Pat Boone to Diane Baker
daughter to the uncle

not in the written version
where Lidenbrock, James Mason,
cites Humphry Davy's false dream
of an absence of heat in the earth
or of women in the world whose
courage is to be left while we men
prepare our descent making
to the steamer *Elleanora* in morning air
observing the smoke
coiling up from her funnel
then to the Phoenix Hotel
where climb to the top of a tower and Uncle says
"Look down well! Take a lesson on the abyss!"
But when murder occurs
a widow appears in green at the Phoenix
in the form of Arlene Dahl who owns
widow's stuff and speaks Icelandic
in this case equipment
(none of this in written version)
buying herself a place in the expedition
along with Hans the local who not speaking English
is in it for the wages as he often makes clear
while saving the asses of his masters.
Side note duck scene and duck as character.

The widow's trove of philosophical instruments:
chronometer, thermometer, compass, night glass,
Ruhmkorff's apparatus, pistols, a pick axe,
spades, shovels, rope ladders, iron spikes, a hatchet, a hammer,

a dozen wedges, beef, biscuits, flasks for the water known to be
buried in the world. As for me, I threw myself
into the pleasure of the trip as we, tourists,
enjoyed the weather, freedom, the desire satisfied
to be in activism of eruptions and explosions of this
region where basalt, tuffs, agglomerates,
and lava create ruins of a fiery nature. I bond
with the widow and long for Diane
lover not cousin as in a still later version a family
not appearing here but in thought.

So round the wide base of the rocks we
like knotted roots of oak and vertical columns
among natives and priests whose strange foods
make us think of Transylvania but we at
Snaefell Volcano are in a real place where
a grand staircase takes us to the summit through
a whirlwind, dust devil or *mistour* so-called
cloud formed by glacial winds.
"Now for the crater!" cries my uncle.

Lava then I see as green and black
as earth blue for air and red
for fire though not burning
now though once darkly.
Seeing one bird or volcano
is refuge they say or relief
but there is no relief
in this adventure for me,

fearful companion who fears
this funnel of liquid fire with
thunder as if I were a bullet
looking down the barrel of a gun

while also we on our backs in the crater
sense the curvature of the earth and
Hans sleeps peacefully in his lava bed.
Thus the first night in the volcano.

Uncle dreams again of Humphry Davy's
theory of chemical heat the cold
fusion of which charms
while failing to be true
unlike me Pat Boone, singing us along the trail
joined by lady love Diane Baker who
finds a way down having heard about Arlene Dahl's
presence in the expedition and about
the famous beauty routines that allow her
to rival the inner glow of her youthful companion,
widow though she is.

We all descend as morning light
on clear rock after quiet shines.
Our breakfast of biscuit washed down with glacial
melt and gin. The journey begins
in earnest 8:17 AM, 43° F, direction down
into quartz gallery set with glassy tears vast
as the *descensus Averni* of Virgil in another volcano

at another time until we stop to
sleep without reflection
and wake to transitional rocks of Silurian System
endlessly cascading through to
the whole of the Carboniferous period
inscribed into a dark space sharp with hydrocarbon
called firedamp by miners who later die but we
lucky men and superadded women
and pet duck who often finds the way
go forward as our Ruhmkorff's devices
light our imaginary day.

Lit but lost we arrive half dead
back at the fissure from whence
that morning and now what
day is it and what use the chronometer?
We proceed through the cracks in the crust
made by displacement, as my uncle
explains, like a rotting apple though we
can't eat ourselves out so wander through
schist and stratified gneiss, the light from
our devices coruscating our way through
hollow diamond and solid sapphire
and my, "Come to me I'm dying!" is noticed
only by Hans who takes an ax to the glassy
wall producing a hiss of steam that cools into
tea of earth as I think of it and
gratefully quench my thirst
at the end of the second day.

It's just a forest of mushrooms, Uncle
claims, another day another explanation
as we, buried alive, go on anyway.
A deadly cold descends from these fleshy
vaults and then prehistoric bones and
a jaw of mastodon and teeth
of Deinotherium giant all around.
"Are we the only thing alive," I cry,
"in this subterranean world or am I asleep
already dreaming this hideous forest, this
vast ocean inside?"

Wind wild with storms and a pink
horizon in all versions an inexplicable glow
neither day nor night and we in a raft,
a craft of fossil wood with blanket
sails like children, set out and fall
asleep careless floating as endless
algae ribbons close around our hearts.
The ship's log kept by me "Steady breeze,
progress in a straight line but to where?"
We catch Devonian fish. Saurians glide by,
a crocodile, a whale, I can see its fins!
Fossils are born again only to die back.
Centuries pass like days I sleep or faint
half sliding into the sea and would have
thrown myself away if not for the restraining
hand of Hans who, noting the time, and despite
the spectacle, asks for his wages. A plesiosaur,

an ichthyosaurus, mortal enemies, tails flopping, make
our hearts stop. Fortuitously we land on what we call
Axel's Island after I, Axel, and a fountain appears,
no, a geyser, in granite mixed with siliceous turf.

"We are underneath England now," I say, calculating as we
set off again. "Let's reef the sail," I cry but, "No! by the Devil,"
shouts my uncle. "Let the wind seize us! Let the storm take
us away. Let me see the rocks of shore though our raft
be smashed!" Rain itself like a sea meets the sea below
boiling now, lightning, thunder, detonations, hailstones,
waves crested with fire. Blinded, stunned I hold to the mast.
All night we live in a constant explosion of despair. Where
are we going? When will it end? The storm doubles down.
Waves rise. Mast and sail are gone. A whitish
blue ball descends. All is magnetized. Our hair on end,
we are covered with tongues of fire, dashed to the shore,
shattered by fatigue, *back where we started.*

Then to marching on layers of bones an immense
Tertiary forest of pines, yews, cypress, a carpet of moss,
flowers with no color or scent as if made of paper.
"Onward!" says my uncle. We find a rust covered dagger
on a granite slab, with the half-eroded name of
Arne Sakmussen and proceeding into a vast tunnel
come to a lost city, the ruins of a Roman town filled
with giant lizards. We run for our lives, pursued by them
and throw ourselves into a wide stone bowl as if for sacrifice.
"We're giving up!" I cried, the water rising under us and

lava also, boiling away the water. "Why don't we die?" I say
as we rise further and faster. "Eruptive granite!" my uncle cries
as if that was an answer, "Gneiss! Mica schist!" We in the Transition
Zone, feel the heat increasing. Are we headed into a furnace?
The walls are burning, the rock molten, the compass wild.

"The mineral crust of the globe never at rest is not resting now,"
he goes on, "Explosions, tectonic movements, alter all
beneath and before us." "But Uncle!" I say, "the crust is about to burst.
We are lost!" "No," he replies, "We're in the chimney of an active volcano."
"Why is that better?" I shout. "It's our way out," he calls. By then I was
not the master of my thoughts. "Look uncle!" I say as the sulfurous
fumes of eruption surround us. "Oh child," he cries, "None of this
is possible!" A column of ash, scoriae and rock fragments float with us
on a flood of lava haloing our heads, our hair on fire, our trousers
burned to our butts, but our hearts are stout as our vessel spins,
rising up through the mountain as it erupts and half-naked we emerge
from a crater sliding on foot down a steep slope, mute
but for Hans who mumbles "Job well done," in Icelandic
but only Arlene Dahl hears him. Trees appear and figs finally
and a child speaking Italian which no one understands but we
hear the word Stromboli and he leads us into town, tourists again,
and then we are home where my uncle, most glorious of savants,
lectures interminably speaking for me and Diane, himself, Arlene,
but not for Hans or the duck.

7.

To the Diamonds (after Newton)

Sulphurous gold-bearing vapor
signals the presence of copper
and gold near the mountainous crown.
Diamonds found also after the glass crackt
and some of the matter (diamonds from inside where)
pressurized carbon forms the hardest substance
(Superman does this in an early episode)
as later sand sticks to hot iron and flows
Active Geothermal Systems and Gold-Mercury Deposits
And mercury is found in local fog

Recent theory of diamonds
Jupiter and Saturn awash in them
floating in liquid hydrogen-helium also
Moon sized one found in constellation Centaurus

When, back to the laboratory,
red dusty Sulphur adhering to the glass
like wax and flew most of it away
resulting in weathered masses of clay
the famous "blue ground"
held over a candle
they flew both away
in the same heat and time
(also called the sublimate)
As ejecta including diamonds
explosively placed by volatile magmas
creates beryl & red emeralds
rarer than diamonds they

form near the surface at low pressure
instead of far below at high

To make a diamond. I, Newton.
Take the whitest flint thou canst get &
beat the outside & dissolve the rest as
much as thou wilt in the white water
& when it is dissolved to clear (not to a pap)
put it into a violl and stop it close
and set in warm ashes & in 12 days
it will congeal to a hard gray
stone then increase the fire that the glass
may be red hot, let it cool & take it out
it will be like flint but polish it
and thou never sawest such a
sparkling diamond or so hard

I, Newton, having been not only a witness
but also an actor of such mysteries
of Nature as the world is not worthy of &
the wise men of the world do scarce believe

the Vultur being upon the mountain
cries with loud voice I am
white of black & red of citrine
An honorable stone which is hidden
In the caverns of the metals
Surely I speak the truth

8.

Lemurian Objects

for CAConrad

Not sand but ash
                human fears (we)
                       forget we are happy
        melting like water like water silver
        babbling
                conical conifers
                  agate eyed
stacking rocks, speak
                  high
                  magnesium
                  and a sight

Volatilized up
from Telos
        Walter Pierson, Mol Lang
                they (we)
                mean with
      each declension
      circumnavigate, tower
                    chat
                    sing
                    flower

Cool until molten inside outside
                    travelling
            Shasta, Shasty, Tschastal
                    big crystal
                    small moon

(We) want to exist
        in actual time
                spindly shrub
                        round hairy leaves
        fallen facts
        thin section of that which
                fat chance

Exhausted, trapped in earth
        whose point of view
                        by the road
                        invisible
                        in our quiet
        Famously our clothes our occasions rhyme with
                        shell amber
                        honey dyed
                        so am I

Afternoon glass of tea
    faceted/aspects of
            tired
            buzzing
            fluttering
            fiery
   crack in the world reveals
   footprint of the avalanche
            exacting
            calls of birds

(We) went back in time
    checked our moon found
        others with same moon
            if not mine
            my feeling (we)
            left nothing behind
   though felt left by the real
        in several rooms in many ways
            people, as a woman on the trail
            space holder
            beheld me (you)

Remembered
winter in the forest

troubled goddess whose
skinny child 6'5"
absurdly blue eyes
appears in your mind
each history different
longing the same

Fabric includes local crystals
smoky quartz
root attached
solar impact
draws breath
replacing it with
you as the nonhuman
intervention

Walter Pierson, Mol Lang intervene
inter-veined sheer
glass plates
false fire   real steam
calms the edges of the door
open in your system the
shadow form of a butte

off to the side
headwaters

Your childhood river on the rise
someone else's religion
leave(s) nothing here (there)
mineralized prism (prison) only
blue rainbow conglomerate
obsidian and cinder
with roseate behavior
of asphalt and rhyolite
finding recognition

Stringed things bring about
estrangement catastrophe
meadow cleared of trees
strange debris where
a woman gathers and protects
no one
suspects her
of being in charge
the title an ironic honorific is

Lost and lost again
solid to liquid
trails begin out of nowhere
                                their music cheerful and virtuosic
their quartz clear their calcite yellow as wings their
                                chromatic range determines
their level of yearning

Fill the cup and dawn occurs
What if science is right and you have
other dimensional matter in your body?
If the mountain sounds
is that the crystal organ?
As she writes we are sitting
by her side telling her everything

Bi-locating silver skinned
                    officials the clear mask
bureaucratic atomistic kinesis
                    ventriloquy you can
                    visit without
being there (here) where

Seeing is reading
our drones   whine while
          past life regression
          legal in the spirit world
produces
hypothetical content continent
another happy day

The matter in your hand
                              volcanic genesis
                                        place spelled backwards
             epoch more or less when
             they say this is California
             what does that mean?
                              Needed dissonance
                                        during the voyage

half-dead pilot
                    plant also nearly gone but
growing brings back the avalanche
                                        glass glissando
                              comes together in your head
                    and on your tongue
                    tiny crystals line up the shards

                split into musings more like
            being high than being low

Daily life underground
                        ideas emerge into gray areas
the horizontal approach
                        evening voices
                        interrupt the continuum
the Clear, the Pitt, the Sacramento, the Cottonwood, the Hat
                        human accessible
only through directed thought
            second and tertiary periods for example
sudden stoppages
                stalagmites
                stalactites
                        local truth
                            subjugated knowledge
discarded sensibilities

The garden Mu or Lemuria
                        utopic or ectopic depression
mentioned at length

                              50,000 years ago again
the lost place
exceeds
                         the loss it evokes
                         Telos City
an ephemeral presence
radical, discontinuous, enchanted, irrevocable,
                              unable to be unsaid, unknown
ending anyway

A place name or eternity of loss
                    some choice
continents drift apart
long periods of repose
moth eaten texture
                    a language
                    begins with a chant
a baby, the oldest script, a village

In this scenario
charity, compassion, nonviolence,
                              sinking landmass, or
                              towering inferno
when sex occurs

lost glory also laughing
brings back the ice age

                accidental discovery
                undermined, overturned,
                rented, gutted, walls, plazas,
                rocks, humans, objects
waves, history

Each day a new flag
Every year pilgrims
escape into the light
pretending to belong to time
An underwater find booms forth
as I dive into the channel
experts at hand huge stones,
cut blocks, crockery, pots, jewels,
Telosian scrolls of poetry

You answer your own question
                I need a flood myth
            an antediluvian domain to stay
hidden in a road through rubble
        Call it my mind my

Mu here the poem is
                    a rectangle embedded in stone
Danger not superstition is the danger
flawed crystal or other forms

Home from the journey
                    unpacked things back
in use at work
in life but not yet
                    voice cracks enable this approach
Trail of mugwort over-dreaming
                    skunk, sage, weeds, heat,
                                        the forest floor series

                    We claim not to displace
beings of another dimension
but realize the idea itself
                    is displacement
our loud longing,
                    brassy beauty and proclivities

close to hell or equally

Distant it is heaven that changes
objects from our story
                        notion of earth mute triumph
explosion stops time
by replicating space
                    No, wait (this is Mol)
                    (Walter) The opposite is the case

            Unafraid of contradiction
                    the mountain
                    is our life
            inside our living room
our stone parts and limitless perception
            erases the question
            who is transcendent
                    to whom
                    in a line meant
                    we transcend together

Lemurian scale said to be unfettered
      is merely elongated
      like our lives and eyes
an exchange of delusions
collapsible atmo of Io
      freezing every "night" to reassemble
           the next "day"
Volcanoes there also

Lemurians can know things
           melting and running away
Walter (I say)
Mol (he responds)   this is sex
           I am blue and translucent
           from (not) existing

We love the mountain
needing room to expand
      A still speaks in our movie
A *List of States and Exaggerations*
      the lava beneath our house
liquid mantle, solid core seethes
           we hollow earth beings childish
      feminine
        senile
          mad

                                        cheap
                        and romantic our voices amped
                        we see them form from

Origin tales into desire lines
          we share each other's fate,
                              rocks
                              towers
                              ire
              our thoughts alight
              our air dims
the usual clowns appear
our witches predict
                              the thin wind dares us
              further in, farther onto
just in time
rituals of desire

          Our crystallinity
          fully flowers
          fucking forth into
Lemurian heaven
          glass bridges,
glass floors, space everywhere

We are in space
This is also work
Blood in our veins totally alive
inside our pink hearts (our skies)

9.

Analogic Geology

Analogic Geology: Lists & Definitions

Volcano as FORM, edifice,
environment, process, event,
genre, or situation typically
erupts lava or melted planet.
A version called CRYOVOLCANO
spews instead ice, water,
mud, ammonia, methane etc.
Terrestrial volcanoes discharge
not only LAVA but carbon monoxide
and dioxide, methane, SULFUR DIOXIDE,
and other poisons as do refineries and
chemical PLANTS as they are called.
These are like volcanoes in the TOXIC
or catastrophic sense and not entirely
unlike the cryovolcanic entities found
in our SOLAR SYSTEM on planets and on
moons as Titan, Ceres (the size of Texas),
Enceladus, on Kuiper Belt Objects, as well
as in Richmond, Rodeo, Crockett, Benicia,
Martinez, Pittsburg and Antioch.
The local OIL COAST is made of five
refineries run by Chevron, Phillips 66, SHELL,
Martinez, Tesoro, Valero, and four
chemical plants operated by Shell, General
Chemical, DOW, and Hasa Inc.
Same in Texas, Louisiana, Utah, Southern
California—in all about 140 major

REFINERIES in the US (also, of
course, more world-wide) where EARTH
becomes a sacrifice zone for pipelines and BIG OIL
as is Standing Rock or maybe not this time.
Energy sources for volcanoes can be radioactive decay
melting from the inside out, tidal friction from
translucent DEPOSITS OF FROZEN
materials, or just business as usual
creating a (sub)surface greenhouse effect
to generate heat or industrial capitalism
to generate wealth. EARTH can be thought
of as a single VOLCANO scaled up. We can
define ourselves geologically, meteorologically
or in whatever nonhuman way we name
this epoch or extinction or whatever this is.
Whoever we are.

Analogic Geology: Toxic Trail

The air is the emergency
or the unnamed spill
in Suisun Bay today which
failing at first to be sourced
(turns out it's CHEVRON) evaporates
driving a few to the hospital
with nausea from a burning
smell coming from the WATER
by way of the refinery
or from TANKERS–extensions
as they are of the industry and
industrial CAPITAL said to have caused
(as I recently read) geology to exist
as a discipline. But, I thought,
geology doesn't cause refineries
any more than chemistry does
except in that the required knowledge
can be seen to be pre-monetized
by the entities that endow its chairs and
hire its workers. It is a strange pleasure
to think that way as I did and do
reminding me of the original sin of my Catholic
youth or the Spicerian fix that's always in.

In 1876 oil was discovered in California
by STANDARD OIL which soon acquires

600 acres in Point Richmond. Standard
was incorporated 1905 but then dismantled
in 1911 into 33 companies in a trust busting
move but was it? The REFINERY's own
history tells how it was critical in WWI
and more so in II. Meanwhile in 1915
automobiles boom. JD ROCKEFELLER
was the richest man in the world. African
American workers arrive from the South
and are hired. Women are hired. Standard
has become Chevron by then, COMPANY
and TOWN are reported by the Richmond Museum
to have been glad together with advanced-for-then
personnel policies, eight-hour days, training etc.
A group of women called the CHEVRONETTES
appeared and were photographed. Today Chevron
LOOMS over bay and town steaming
night and day toxically up into the horizon

not completely unlike having say
MOUNT RAINIER an hour from Seattle—
big beautiful mountain you can ski and hike
and gaze at it but if Rainier goes it takes the town.
Though maybe not good to make such a comparison
as God or whatever makes volcanoes
or geology or tectonics does or the GODDESS.
Anyway volcanoes are not part of CAPITALISM
except as everything is or in how resources
are used but in their sublime power are

not always usable and can be catastrophe itself
as also earthquakes more common so more feared are
seen as planetary powers—EARTH, wind, and fire—
not as evil but as forces of NATURE as people
are sometimes called that and CAPITAL
has that reputation or is ascribed
that inevitability. If you regulate, reps of
VALERO say, they will be forced out of California
to a less regulated state where they will
contribute more to global warming.
Seriously, that was the argument along
with their having already fixed the problem
(mainly operator error, natch) resulting
in the two hundred grand fine otherwise
known as the cost of doing business,
as we in business say.

Refineries are not the only elements of the toxic trail.
Famously, ZENECA Agricultural Products, a chemical
plant on the bay near MEEKER SLOUGH and
STEGE MARSH, was cemented over in an unregulated
clean-up that ultimately ravaged now activist
Sherry Padgett. She ran an electrical cable business
across the street and *swept up* poison dust intentionally
spread near her business before the CEMENTING
after which rare bone and thyroid CANCERS
hollowed out her small frame. Other residents
had other cancers but cancer is rarely connectable
to the cause of cancer, as any lawyer will tell you.

The BAY TRAIL includes this cemented site
surrounded also by a chain link fence with warning signs.
Nearby are duck-filled lagoons formerly called
Chemical Pond A and Chemical Pond B where
arsenic, lead, zinc, and mercury once degraded
to become even more toxic. Also sulfuric acid as in
gasses from volcanoes which is why it can be
dangerous to go out in a boat near Kīlauea
in Hawaii to see the LAVA because it's not benign
as one might imagine or hope the TOURISTIC
SUBLIME reliably to be.

But let's talk about sublimes. RICHMOND is more
quotidian than SUBLIME in its toxicity
with the genuinely TOXIC SUBLIME truer, for my
money, of other sites such as the leaden white pools
of the MALAKOFF DIGGINS, now a state park,
a century after they were created by gold miners
in the nearby foothills of the Sierra Nevada
still part of the drainage of the Sacramento Delta.
Or one pictures CHERNOBYL. The raising
of the level of the SACRAMENTO RIVER by six feet
of mud during the Gold Rush is not nothing though
in Ukraine there is that no-people rule and the
half-life of poison on a COSMIC SCALE.

There are other SUPERFUND SITES, as they are called,
in California and in America but, as Sherry Padgett
points out, there is no Superfund or funds

of any kind and so no incentive to clean the Zeneca
site which has not surprisingly not happened
though the place is part of an upscale housing development
and state park and is almost as BUCOLIC these
days as Chernobyl appears in rhapsodic selfies.

You are often on the TOXIC TRAIL when you hike
in the East Bay Regional Park if, as I, you frequently
do that kind of thing. Such hiking is a bit like conceptual
art in that it provides many chances
to observe, investigate, and participate in
these toxicities, importantly not limited to Richmond,
which has, however, well more than its share.
LIFE and NON-LIFE is the subject. More on that.
The Bay Trail is a formal and historical construct
as well as an actual trail which follows the outline of the
San Francisco and San Pablo Bays. One notes
on the map of such things that there are no toxic hot sites
in the upscale Marin County sections of the trail.

Unlike, again, Richmond where TERRA NOVA
is the phrase ornately used on the signage
at the West Contra Costa County Sanitary Landfill
visible from my window as a manmade PROMONTORY
and where I sometimes go. This closed disposal site
for HAZARDOUS WASTE is being treated with layers
of topsoil, gravel, plastic, compacted clay, UNNAMED
wastes, liquid leachate, and bay mud—all said not to allow
drainage to the bay. It's a three-mile hike amidst

pickleweed, crows, derelict boats, tires, Marbled
Godwits, Sandpipers, Long-billed Curlews, Greater
White-fronted Geese, and magnificent Turkey
Vultures which land before you only to take lazily off
as you pass by. There are often smoky fires
at the top of the GARBAGE MOUNTAIN as it is
called in still other signage around which
you walk burning God knows what unspeakable
detritus. Adjacent to the park is the Golden Bear
Transfer Station or dump where one actively brings
big and/or toxic things and pays to leave them.
It is an easy though mentally challenging hike which
affords excellent views of the Chevron Refinery
a few hundred yards across the bay. Turning
your back on it you encounter a chemically
bright green LAGOON filled with American White and
Brown pelicans, Mallards, American Wigeons, and
Green-winged Teals. Further signage points out
that wetlands are the KIDNEYS OF THE BAY,
filtering pollutants from urban runoff. There are
solar power collectors to your right as you arrive
back at the parking lot where you usually find yourself
alone or with one other car and might think
as I have, well it's better than it was, but is it?

Analogic Geology: Daily Life

LIFE and NON-LIFE are the OBJECTS interacting
as they create the strata that will define
our time whether anyone is here to read it or not.
As I read and weep someone not me stares
into a device believing lies with a heart
damaged by ECONOMIC VIOLENCE.

At what level of action is agency felt by the actor?
STANDING ROCK SIOUX and many others in a convocation
of TRIBES larger than any since the nineteenth century
put themselves on the line as WATER PROTECTORS.
They pray and sing. Others donate and call.
Watch and pray. I guess this is PRAYER.
I educate myself when a man who is there
is asked what others who are not there
can do and he says "EDUCATE YOURSELF."
People with MONEY and TIME go to witness,
document and, briefly, share the danger.
The DANGER seems terrible as I write.
Veterans arrive as HUMAN SHIELDS but can they?
Thomas Lopez of the International Youth Council,
Standing Rock Sioux Chairman Dave Archambault,
and others speak at the press conference.
There is a softness to their speech and demeanor.
I can't figure out all of their names.
As I write I read that Obama has
denied the permit for the DAKOTA ACCESS PIPELINE.

People cheer and in the same breath
fear the decision might not last
because of the DISASTER of the last election.
DAILY LIFE unites and divides us.
We are the physical variable in the exchange of
information between ourselves and the EARTH.
"WE ARE NOT VICTIMS" It is the same world.
A movement built on land, power, and bodies scatters
like glass into nonrepetitive shards multiple, singular,
clear and sharp. Bright like the ice there today
but unlike ice "Don't melt away."

10.

Slant Range

after Bruce Conner

His Head

The man's face is a slant range.
He is an artist and a collage,
a semblance of VOLCANOES, sky and clouds.
His is a volcanic art its subject
a molten scene filled with danger
to the real-life observer as myself
taking this shot in the momentary
absence of museum guards threatened
only by admonishment and the impending
dictatorship. The two visible VOLCANOES
in this portrait are made of lines
and crosshatching. They are assembled
though the artist pictured is a painter
whose palette is prominently displayed.
His is a constructive art. His paint is made of thought.
Dressed like a MOUNTAIN or in MOUNTAINS
his MOUNTAINOUS head reveals the substantiality
of his thinking. There is nothing visible about his heart.

EXPLO EXPO

A Bomb; Atomic veteran; Acute Exposure;
Base Surge when a cloud EXPLODES
from the bottom of a column
formed by a subsurface EXPLOSION as in
the 1945 Crossroads tests transformed
by Bruce Conner into a film of the same name
in 1976. By chance the same year capitalism

failed though we didn't know it then. One could
watch this movie over and over during museum hours
until two days after the above-mentioned
dictatorship began or was it a *coup d'état*?
Condensation Cloud–the signature
formation–consists of water droplets
resulting from a negative phase of
the blast wave; Contamination self-explained;
Fallout; Fireball; Firestorm from childhood
nightmares; H for hydrogen (bomb for bomb);
Half-life; First Strike; Fusion; Gun-type Weapon;
High Altitude Burst; IMPLOSION; Kiloton; Irradiate;
Lethal Dose; Neutron Bomb; Nuclear Winter we
worried about decades ago during the reign of
another president who we also perceived as dangerous
and who was; Overpressure is pressure in excess
of normal atmosphere in pounds per square inch
as in physical effects of the EXPLOSION
where buildings are demolished, people killed;
Photon; Proton; Rad as unit of absorbed radiation;
Rainout as removal from a radioactive cloud of
particles by precipitation, see "A Hard Rain's A-Gonna Fall";
Roentgen a unit of exposure; Rosenberg case equals
more death; Scaling Law when effects are determined
as a function of distance from the EXPLOSION–requires
a reference EXPLOSION; Single Integrated Operation Plan
(SIOPS) tells how nukes should be used in a given situation;
Hanford, Oakridge, and Los Alamos are W, X and Y;
Slant Range the distance from the EXPLOSION

to the observer; Subsidence Crater from an EXPLOSION
close to the surface; Supercritical the level achieved
when things EXPLODE; Strategic as a word and
concept often connected with the idea of Tactical
referring in turn to battlefield nukes–which "What?";
Thermal Energy emitted from an EXPLOSION; Thermal
Radiation ultraviolet, visible, or infrared; Transmutation
converts one element to another through bombardment;
Transuranic; Triad; Trinity Test; Tritium; Thermonuclear
Weapons where fission produces fusion; Warhead the
part that EXPLODES; Weaponization is just what we do;
X Rays or also Thermal X Rays at millions of degrees
following the EXPLOSION; Yellowcake, mostly
uranium where acid is drained from the crushed ore,
really is yellow; Yield the total effective energy released
during the EXPLOSION; Zero Sum EXPLOSION
convinces no one of nothing.

BOMBHEAD

No one has died of radiation poisoning
yet from events at Fukushima. Plant
owner, Tepco, wants to bring it back online
convinced that people will continue
not to die. But the prefecture and people
elsewhere are not so sure despite
the fire trucks lined up and redundant
power supplies and the frozen wall beneath
which the waste, failing to freeze, as was

the plan, is failing to keep the radiation
in check at the site in a breathtaking
example of too much too late.
Folks, unable to get that
radioactivity out of their heads,
oppose the possible impossible
EXPLOSION because they know
they must share the air,
or lack of it, as if with one head
or one LARGE DEATH.

II.

Personal Volcanoes

A FULLY enfranchised
semi-inexhaustible
nonhuman assemblage not entirely
alive but not dead except as all rocks might be
said to be nonalive though the processes sought
by those searching for life are not absent from their actions
when they are ACTIVE as opposed to DORMANT so-called because
the time they occupy is so much larger than ours that even a sudden
move on their part might seem NOT to have occurred at all from our
perspective in spite of its impact on our lives and on LIFE ON EARTH as we call it when
we talk about how everything changes and what that means about how we are FUCKED

OPEN
at the top
self-constructed of DETRITUS
hardened into a temporary
tower or pyramidal entity with
communication options unlike speech though
articulate enough in their expression of facts
of LIFE potentially deadly to the alive thing and to
the sense of stability the living like to ascribe to the ground
we walk on or the mountains as solid as mountains we look up TO

As BREATH
forms GLASS from melted
SAND breath of magma to lava (erupts) and
by chance brings ruby, beryl, sapphire, & diamonds from
depths and JET, the mourning stone, lignite, or petrified wood
as obsidian is petrified light (KNIFE) bereft of crystal HIGH in silica
GLASS is hard, brittle, sharp can be a weapon or polished and rounded as the
present GLOBE of snowflake obsidian on the writing table. We are surrounded by stone as silicon
dioxide is granite or rhyolite though GLASS isn't crystal but the product of air and congealed liquid
faceted with convergent TIME and SPACE as the GLASS dome or conservatory, spectacle of global
capital, science, and LOCAL despair. There is NOTHING else there but impenetrable miles of DARK
strata concealing the HEART inside
and the KNIFE

PILE as
heap or HOARD
extending in all directions
bed, plain, or field of LAVA−moss
covered in the present instance cold wind
more GOLD than green cushioning and breaking down
the already broken stretch allowing one to rest in cool SUN also sea
everywhere visible from this ISLAND or anyway often as moments stop but
continue open endedly to reflect back when soaking in SULPHUR bath
found in most rented places here where water and heat are abundant

not from the sun but from the CENTER each plate end to end
of world to world producing mountains or ridges or seeps
steaming each an OMPHALOS but can there
be more than one or more than many
CENTERS?

The TOUR
shows where
erosion reaches
into LAVA fashioning
secondary minerals as
pitchstone, olivine, rhyolite,
or anything into the FORM of a
xenolith like ourselves foreign OBJECTS hurtling
through space and time detached from what was
never attached to anything anyway not knowing how NOT

to be unlike these ROCKS whose anomaly is inscribed with traces of
ORIGIN barely legible as people related simply by being PEOPLE including ones
not looking like each other or themselves as we, self-pictured BLOBS of light and stone,
reflect what is obvious about being alive in a place with few locals, a million visitors, and no
NIGHT at times or at times only us, them, and DARKNESS surrounded by water surrounded by
continents and ICE mountains blue on top and invisibly VAST beneath what to us (me) is the last identity
but one already lost before connecting to the past you raise
your SHIELD and hold your SWORD as if there was a defense against the namelessness we share which
with glacial quickness apprehends the unimaginable end of the TOUR
ecstatic BRAIN in geothermal pool BLUE with use

A PHREATIC eruption
answers the question
'Where do you go?'"
boiling steam as clothes
to make for the Snowcat
a complex stratovolcano
the height of Lassen Peak
which however is a lava
rose, pyroclastic material
new craters generating a
eruption that reached
Ash Advisory connected
a subdued PAROXYSM.
the journalist said who
despite being pelted
burned coat tweeted

when groundwater explodes
"When lava hits the ice and snow
Dodging rocks, burning boulders,
melt, heads are hit it's good
honking in the steam. Mount Etna,
like Mount Shasta but shorter, is more
 at just over ten thousand feet
dome. Suddenly the tremor steeply
poured from between the old and
rheomorphic lava flow in a Strombolian
the base of the cone. There is an
to this event which could be called
"I thought we were going to die!"
kept her camera rolling
with red hot ejecta as shown by the
soon after the EXPLOSION

RED ROCK CINEMA presents THE VOLCANO SHOW being the adventures of VILLI KNUDSEN who, with cats Voltaire and Mocha, occupies the two red cottages of the cinema complex in a courtyard down the street from our Airbnb. Mocha is excessively friendly if allowed to join you for the screening. Voltaire is absent. We are unable to pay in cash and bond with Villi when, after the films, we wander out in search of money at the local BONUS. He seems frail but isn't but IS compared to the younger self you see in the movies which along with the catastrophes recorded there remind one of DEATH and AGE and the despair that might or might not be brought by cataclysm. Villi seems a wily old VIKING particular to his place and time. When I mention Cascade volcanoes he dismisses them as inferior to Icelandic ones. Like those of his father, his films present waiting, occasional EXPLOSIONS, and various near fatal events, not always volcanic in nature, as when in ecstatic response to an eruption, he reaches over and turns off the engine of the small plane he's in and the pilot says never do that again but not long after he does. In the tradition of the sagas these realistic docs are not mythic but telling of the story of waiting, viewing, and surviving seismic events. Islands form, towns are consumed, lava emerges from a miles long

fissure not so far from where we are sitting (given that we have come here from California). In this personal museum, basalt, crystal, lava samples, and piles of powdery SULPHUR are displayed in the window sills among film canisters, brochures, and the homey smells of old man and cats. The thickly painted boulder in the courtyard with its RED ROCK logo of stylized fire in a chalice in a square could be, I think, the picture of the contents of my HEAD where I share an interest with Villi though he can't recognize it or sees but knows I am an amateur at the obsession for which he has never stinted and even now is napping in the cot next to the door or introducing his own films and demanding cash and wandering out into the familiar town dreaming of silence and subglacial ERUPTION, flash floods, lava flow, cash, and waiting.

PYROGLYPHS
by Steina in collab Tom Joyce
the FIRE part of a chart in which
molten metal comprises the WATER
of this installation where I see in retrospect the
bench where I left my bag in the video DARK running
when remembering back from the over-lit café upstairs then
staying to WATCH and listen again to varieties of FLAMES and sounds from
smelting I always say it's not the lava but maybe it is the crashing and hissing
filled with DANGER only if you are present or if you fail to hang onto your bag staying as I
did at the beginning of what turned out to be a CONTINUUM WITH watching Bruce Conner's
bomb explode repeatedly STAYING on the surface of myself liking to find there a personal IMPLOSION

pulling APART
at a fingernail rate of
growth as any alive thing
spreading out to make the Atlantic Ocean until
islands (Ísland) and mountains form feeling unlike the
right-lateral strike-slip MOTION we have been taught to imagine
occurs beneath California or the violently SUBDUCTIVE displacement of the
Cascades with its massive earthquakes and EXPLODING mountains which however
also occur here (THERE) as a context for much else functioning as an ENGINE that heats
the world and increases it adding to the LITHO, ATMO, and other spheres in ways that can
be measured but can't be stopped or almost never though even that ONCE

COLUMNS
of
basalt
far
down
into
LAVA
cooled
and
shrunken
becoming
pavement
SIX-
sidedly
as when
mud in
drought
or BEES
in hives

basalt
AGAIN
next to
a penny
glassy
common
dark
massive
MAFIC
igneous
rhyo-
lite
LIGHT
white

molten
flood pre-
Cascade
but local
to this
coastal
HOT
spot as
Iceland
migrates
northwest or
Northern
Ireland
Giants
Causeway
LINGERS
dissolving

when
SIDES
fit against
each
flat or
rugged
as olden
other
muck
ugly
words of
Old Norse
heathen
skull
die
knife
TROLL
thing

snare
litmus
that
poorly
recorded
hoard of
inter
locking
towers of
dregs
mired
rotten
berserk
gift of
slaughter
law
loan
bug
reindeer
wing
bleak
sky

without
warning
a crevice
opens
MOLTEN
ignites
destroying
house
streets
TOWN
but was
stopped by
PEOPLE
firemen with
hoses rocks
and stuff just
PEOPLE who
however
can't always
or even
OFTEN
succeed
in stopping
anything

12.

Finally the Eye

GRAVESNAME

SPACE
GLASS
ACTION
VOLCANO
LOVE
EARTH
DISASTER
HOLLOW
ACCELER-
ATION
AN
THROW
POE
SEEN
YEARS
TERRANE
TERRAIN
TECTONIC
PLATE
LAYER
CAKE
TEARS
MOUNTAIN
MARS
ASH
HOLLOW
EARTH

If grave is place divided by
time with CIRCULAR and
ELEVATED layers where we
(they) pile up, dance, dig, die,
turn, burn, and PASS through

the light including BONES not
always ours we become realigned
objects of desire as cows and
bulls falling prey to our (their)
LOVE of cattle and belief

in an afterlife whose nameless
ancestors also dead but present
remind us that one escorts the other
into the SPACE where we write
a new name on an old rock.

Mist drifts up or is it SMOKE
from burned bones or is it just
the grassy top of the MOUND we
are on where spiralized mountains
flatten to be written onto stones?

Dragged ton by ton as generations'
WORK, now surround the handmade
butte we circumnavigate following signs

CHEVRON
MOUNT
RAINIER
GODDESS
CAPITALISM
VALERO
MEKER
SLOUGH
STEGE
MARSH
BAY
TRAIL
LAVA
TOXIC
SUBLIME
CHERNOBYL
TOXIC
TRAIL
LIFE
NON-LIFE
TERRA
NOVA
PROMONTORY
TURKEY
VULTURES
GARBAGE
MOUNTAIN

ECONOMY
GOD
PYRAMID
FLEXURE
THERE
PLACE
FACE
GRAVEL
ASH
CLOUD
OMEN
MOUNTAIN
OBJECTS
FACE
FRACKING
FRACK
ENCLOSED
DIRT
SUN
NOT
VOLCANIC
ERUPTION
JUDGE-
MENT
DAY
FACE
PYRO-
CLASTIC
CLOUD

readable formally only as stars again
align omening our past. Our future

begins as any circular problem
becomes fossilized in millennia of
rain and wind and BRAINS from those
heads we found whose memories
pour out or was it SMOKE again

or is it mist as yes missed painfully those
gone ones who were something to
someone long ago or who now comprise
those flattened scratchings on the
stones we rolled and laid out like

tables with such hazard to ourselves
or like boards with paraphernalia of
games or wizard tools legible to
anyone dead but not otherwise
part of the LIFE we haven't left

but will yet, circling back puffing
and playing against clump, cloud,
and cluster of EARTH searching
for the gateway moment when this
trip brings us to our senses or up short

becoming legible. Realizing these
passage graves are volcanoes and we are

LAGOON
KIDNEYS
BAY
LIFE
NON-LIFE
STRATA
ECONOMIC
VIOLENCE
STANDING
ROCK
SIOUX
PRAYER
EDUCATE
YOURSELF
MONEY
TIME
DANGER
HUMAN
SHIELDS
SPEAK
SPEECH
DAKOTA
ACCESS
PIPELINE
DAILY
LIFE
OURSELVES
EARTH
VICTIMS

BAROQUE	in love with them and the language we	SLANT
POST VOLCANO	hear, see, and know nothing of except	RANGE
PRESENT	we do sort of know its sound including speech	VOLCANOES
NATURE		CLOUDS
AIR	but not discluding wood, skin, strings, breath,	SKY
OF	and arrangements of the above with some	PRESENT
EARTH	consideration of STONE as we stand	VISIBLE
EXPLOSION	waiting for the big wagon bus to return	VOLCANOES
MONUMENT	you (us) with the other passengers to	PAINT
ANTHRO-		MOUNTAIN
TURBATION	your life's WORK where you may detect	VISIBLE
ERUPTS	significance in whatever TIME allows SPACE	HEART
WE	for considering us as you or we as those	EXPLO
DARE	unknown builders of these GRAVES so-called	EXPO
YOU	at least by me here included in the random	EXPLODES
TO		EXPLOSION
LISTEN	presence of the LIVING and glad of it	IMPLOSION
RANDOM	thinking of birth seeing the passage	EXPLOSION
COSMO-	as a canal and the form as PERSONAL	EXPLOSION
LOGICAL	MOUNTAIN or the MOUND as VOLCANO	EXPLOSION
FORCES	famously male and female, hollow,	EXPLOSION
EARTH		EXPLODE
ACCEL-	and erect, giving out and taking in	EXPLOSION
ERATE	or wearing down while tourists escape	EXPLODES
OBJECTS	from their tours to fall asleep on the green	EXPLOSION
COMETS	top which is forbidden but they are children	EXPLOSION
VOLCANOES	or Americans and don't know better.	EXPLOSION
PERSIST		RADIATION
POISON	There are no flags here but for family	POISONING

EARTH	or clan or tribe with rules about LAND	EXPLOSION
IRREVERS	and every action or future imagined in the	FULLY
IBILITY	new version of the old engravings illegible	ACTIVE
ANIMAL	now but then were the law or something	DORMANT
EARTH		NOT
EPA	like chevrons, zigzags, lozenges, parallel lines	LIFE
OUTER	meant intensely to their readers and to their dead.	ON
EAST	Are your dead under you or mine under me or	EARTH
BAY	in the air where scattered pyroclastically	FUCKED
WORLD	GRIEF burns down through the EARTH	OPEN
VOLCANO		DETRITUS
VACATION	coming back up as an altered place where	TO
EARTH	REBIRTH rituals of rise and descent arrive	BREATH
QUAKES	and leave adding to the monument until	GLASS
FAR	forgotten again, it is private land, and then	SAND
NORTH	pasture and park celebrant of nothing but	JET
EARTH		KNIFE
EARTH	the unknown past until again discovered	HIGH
SUN	and druids come but even the real ones were	GLASS
ROCKS	CELTS and this grave old when they appeared.	GLOBE
EARTH	But I am no DRUID and you, my interlocutor,	GLASS
THERA	and tour guide are five thousand miles,	TIME
MOUNT		SPACE
PELÉE	mounds of EARTH, and bad and good	GLASS
FATHER	governments away–this to you unknown	LOCAL
GEOLOGY	and possibly as illegible as the GRAVEN symbols	NOTHING
VESUVIUS	drawn out here, written there, and read	DARK
WORLD	in a future where we, as is often said,	HEART
		KNIFE

ARLENE
DAHL
CHEVRON
WATER
TANKERS
CAPITAL
SPICERIAN
FIX
STANDARD
OIL
REFINERY
COMPANY
TOWN

can picture the end of the WORLD but not of
CAPITALISM. But let's celebrate anyway by
visiting these MOUNDED remnants and revenants
and falling in LOVE with the guide, yourself, who
points out the inconsistency of the bright wall

that separates the living from the dangerous
dead and by believing something about the
present where the MOUND is a CLOCK as well
as mountain and we CAPITALIZE for emphasis
and love and there is a future and it is OURS not
HOURS.

PILE
HOARD
LAVA
GOLD
ISLAND
SULPHUR
CENTER
OMPHALOS
CENTERS
TOUR
LAVA
FORM
OBJECTS
NOT

Finally the EYE

Finally the EYE
with its opening
and vitreous gel

sparkling now in
my old self like
an ERUPTION at night

Veined, occluded,
OBSTRUCTED, but
strangely sharper

Age making VISION
clear in a way it
wasn't before though

As with CATARACTS or
gates closing in a castle
narrows the information

Flow while projecting
something like light or life
suggesting the EYE and SELF

Are not DORMANT but ACTIVE
in the head round like
the unthinking world

Acting effectively
but WITHOUT INTENT
unlike I (us) who see

What we want always
BLIND to something
peering out

From STRUCTURES similar
to cats and birds and
other worldly seers

whose EYES are not
like VOLCANOES but for being
of this place and alive

ACKNOWLEDGEMENTS

"Erupting Light" is from the album *Without Sinking* by Hildur Guðnadóttir. Thank you to Manuel Brito, editor and publisher of *The Canary Island Connection* (Zasterle Press), Kent MacCarter of the *Cordite Poetry Review*, Carol Dorf of *Talking Writing*, and Solomon Rino and Colin Partch of *Second Stutter*, who published some of these poems, and to Guy Bennett of Mindmade Books who published the chapbook *Verne & Lemurian Objects*. Thank you also to Nick Robinson with whom I shared all of the considerable onsite volcano research that informed this project.

Laura Moriarty's recent books include *Verne & Lemurian Objects*, *The Fugitive Notebook*, and *Who That Divines*. Her awards include Poetry Center Book Award, a Wallace Alexander Gerbode Foundation Award in Poetry, a New Langton Arts Award in Literature, and a Fund for Poetry grant. She lives in Richmond, California.

NIGHTBOAT BOOKS

Nightboat Books, a nonprofit organization, seeks to develop audiences for writers whose work resists convention and transcends boundaries. We publish books rich with poignancy, intelligence, and risk. Please visit nightboat.org to learn about our titles and how you can support our future publications.

The following individuals have supported the publication of this book. We thank them for their generosity and commitment to the mission of Nightboat Books:

Kazim Ali
Anonymous
Jean C. Ballantyne
Photios Giovanis
Amanda Greenberger
Anne Marie Macari
Elizabeth Motika
Benjamin Taylor
Jerrie Whitfield & Richard Motika

Nightboat Books gratefully acknowledges support from the National Endowment for the Arts and the Topanga Fund, which is dedicated to promoting the arts and literature of California.